Instant Idea Book

Managing Your Classroom!

for Elementary Teachers

- Let's Get Organized
  (pages 5-24)

- Parent Communication Counts
  (pages 25-44)

- Classroom Management Tactics That Really Work
  (pages 45-62)

(includes reproducible pages)

by
Barbara Jean Gruber

illustrations
Ed Salmon

Copyright© 1983 Frank Schaffer Publications, Inc.
All rights reserved · Printed in the U.S.A.
Published by **Frank Schaffer Publications, Inc.**
1028 Via Mirabel, Palos Verdes Estates, California 90274

ISBN #0-86734-048-7

Table of Contents

Let's Get Organized!

Organize your work area, your materials and yourself! With these quick and useful ideas, you can eliminate those "treasure hunts" for lost papers. Plus, you will learn how to make the most of teacher aides and helpers.

Students should learn to share the responsibility for learning. On the following pages, you'll find a host of sure-fire techniques for eliciting competent student help.

Do Something Nice for Yourself --- You Deserve It!

Add some extra touches to your classroom and make it a special place!

- Buy or make a soft, colorful cushion for your chair.

- Bring a small, electric, hot-water pot to school so you can make coffee, tea, hot chocolate or soup during your breaks.

- Bring a radio to school. Enjoy listening to your favorite station when students are not present.

- Instead of making phone calls or doing paperwork during recess breaks, sit back and relax. You deserve a break too! Why not read a magazine, chat with friend or watch the clouds go by?

- Invest in a paper cutter if your classroom is far from the office.

- Hang a mirror in your closet. A car-visor mirror with adhesive strips will stick to the door. Keep a hairbrush and make-up kit near the mirror.

- Keep an extra umbrella and sweater in your closet for unexpected, nasty weather!

- Leave an extra chair next to your desk. When students want to talk with you, they can wait quietly until you acknowledge them. Eliminates interruptions!

- Put an attractive poster on or inside your closet door and set a healthy, green plant on your desk.

- Enlarge your work area by putting another desk or table next to yours. Ask the custodian to adjust the height of the extra desk to the same height as your desk. You'll enjoy your new, executive-sized desk!

- Buy an inexpensive, wire-mesh basket to hang on your closet rod. Keep your keys and whistle in the basket. No more searching through purse or pockets!

Organize Your Work Area

Spend a few minutes getting organized -- you'll be glad you did! No more frantic searching for misplaced items; you'll have everything at your fingertips. Try these helpful tips for easy, instant organization:

- Label six manila folders: Monday, Tuesday, Wednesday, Thursday, Friday and Next Week. Store the folders in a shoe box which you can leave in a desk drawer. If you have a report prepared for the faculty meeting on Wednesday, for example, file it in your Wednesday folder. File all materials which you plan to use next week in the Next Week folder. This simple idea works like magic -- no more treasure hunts for lost papers.

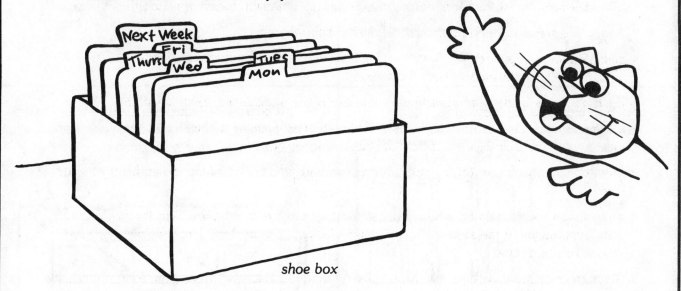

shoe box

- Label enough manila folders for each school month and keep them in your file cabinet (under "M" for months) or in the desk drawer that contains your folders for each day of the week. Now all your ideas and materials will be organized by month.

- If you make a list of things to do at the beginning of the school year, don't throw it away. File it in your September folder and use the list again next year.

Organizing your work area

Use **plastic vegetable bins** for organizing papers.

Label bins:

Take to Office →

Take Home →

File →

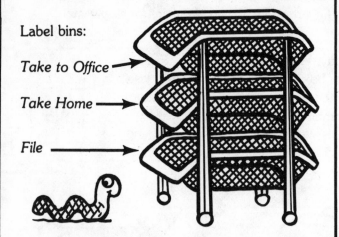

A **wire record rack** keeps important items at your fingertips.

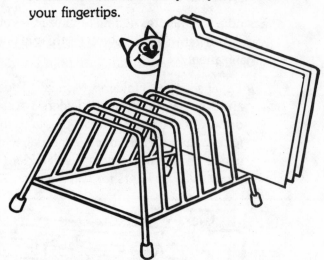

A **shoe bag** is handy for storing:

- scissors
- tape
- stapler
- keys
- coffee mug
- felt pens

This **corrugated cardboard storage file** has cubbyholes for storing books, papers and stacks of worksheets. (Can be purchased in variety and discount stores.)

12″ × 13″

Plastic carryalls are convenient for carrying supplies from place to place in your classroom.

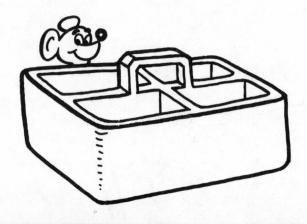

Corrugated cardboard storage boxes are sturdy containers for all sorts of materials.

Dinosaur Unit

Organizing your teaching materials

Color Coding

Label storage areas so materials will be put in the right places. Color coding can help non-readers. For example, a large red dot or strip of red tape on the reading shelf and a red dot on each reading game tells students where each game is stored. Use a different color for each skill (i.e., purple for math, green for language arts, etc.).

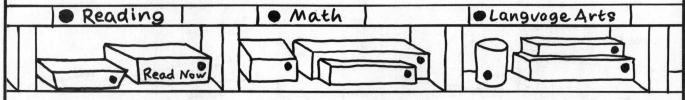

Organize by Topic

Keep all materials for a specific topic together. For example, use a large box for **everything** that belongs with your dinosaur unit. Put duplicating books, ideas from magazines, plastic dinosaur models, bulletin board ideas, patterns to trace and a list of films and books in a box marked Dinosaur Unit. Everything you need will be in one spot.

Shoe Box Survival Kit

Make a shoe box survival kit to keep in your mailbox. Include a pen, pencil, blank duplicating masters, scissors, a class list with student phone numbers and other items that will come in handy when you are away from your desk. Eliminates dashing back to your classroom when you need something! (You might want to keep your box a secret so other teachers are not tempted to "borrow" items. Label the box "Science Continuum" and no one will touch it. Works like magic!) Keep another survival kit in your classroom closet. Include items that you only need occasionally: hammer, nails, cup hooks, screwdriver, can opener, etc.

Something Borrowed

Start a Borrowed List to keep track of items colleagues borrow from you. Staple a piece of paper on the inside back cover of your grade book or plan book. When someone borrows your hammer or a duplicating book, write down the borrower's name and what was borrowed. Cross off the entry when the item is returned.

Organizing your teaching materials

Organize by Skill

File materials by skill. For example, if you have a book of duplicating masters that contains worksheets on synonyms, antonyms and homonyms, tear out the pages and file them according to skill. When your class is working on synonyms, for example, simply pull out your synonym file; it will contain all your materials related to that skill. No more searching through duplicating books for a particular worksheet. When your materials are all organized in one place, you'll be sure to use them.

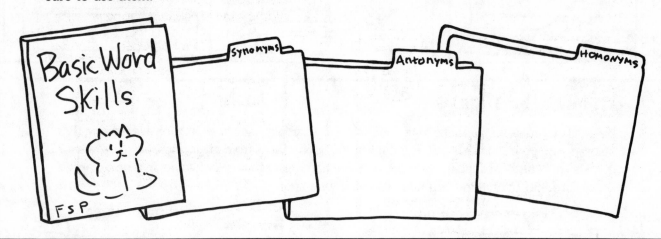

File, File, File

Make folders for everything! If you are planning to teach a weather unit but lack ideas, start a folder marked Weather Unit. When you see a relevant magazine article, tear it out and file it in your Weather Unit folder. As ideas occur to you, jot them down and file them in the folder. When you are ready to write a lesson plan for the unit, you will already have a folder that contains some ideas.

Class Directory

Use three copies of your class list to make telephone directories. Ask students to write their phone numbers next to their names on each class list. Take one list home, put one in your office survival kit (see page 9) and staple the third list inside the cover of your plan book or grade book. What a time saver—eliminates looking up numbers in the phone book!

Be Prepared!

Make sure you're ready for new students. At the beginning of the school year, prepare two or three extra desks. When you duplicate worksheets or prepare a packet or contract, make a few extras.

Organizing your teaching materials

Floor Plan

If you like the way the furniture is arranged in your classroom, quickly sketch the "floor plan" for future use. File your sketch in a folder marked Floor Plans. When you decide to re-arrange the room, look at your floor plan ideas.

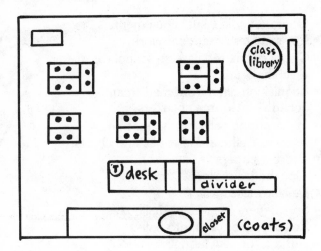

Seating Chart

Make a seating chart to go with each floor plan. It is especially handy when you only want to change the seats of a few students. You can move the names around to make sure the new seating arrangement is workable before you actually move the students. Save time by cutting apart a class list for name slips.

12" × 18" Paper

3" × 5" cards pasted on

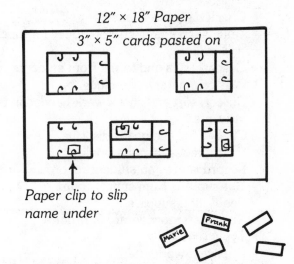

Paper clip to slip name under

Helper Desk

Set up a special desk, table or work area for student helpers. They will appreciate having a "spot" to call their own and you will have a place to leave tasks for your helpers.

Supplies for Helper Desk:
- *class lists*
- *pens & pencils*
- *stapler*
- *sign-in sheet*
- *note pad*

To Do Board

Consider making a To Do bulletin board for your helpers.(Use a small section of one of your bulletin boards). Write tasks to be completed on slips of paper and post them on the To Do board. After each task is finished, the note is removed. Leave two boxes next to the bulletin board for Work to Do and Completed Work.

Your Helper Desk (shown to the left) should be located near the To Do board.

Student helpers and teacher aides

Many parents are unable to spend time helping at school. Why not give them tasks to do at home? Take a look at the following list. Starred items can be completed by parents at home.

How Aides/Parents Can Help

CLERICAL ASSISTANCE:

- Check daily attendance.
- Take lunch count, collect money for lunch and milk.
- Collect notes and forms from students.
- Pass out materials to students.
- Collect, sort and check work handed in by students.
- Change bulletin-board displays.
- Enter grades in grade book.
- Record scores on student records.
- Get supplies from supply room.
- Requisition supplies.
- Keep classroom library in order.
- Typing. ★
- Duplicate worksheets.
- Cut paper for art projects. ★

- Operate audio-visual equipment.
- File samples of student work.
- Check out materials from school library for teaching a unit.
- Requisition films from media center.
- Schedule resource speakers.
- Make phone calls for the teacher. ★
- Prepare flash cards, games and charts. ★
- Correct papers. ★
- Alphabetize materials. ★
- Deliver messages.
- Sort papers in student mailboxes.
- Roll skeins of yarn into balls. ★
- Cut and/or sew fabric. ★
- Proofread teacher-made worksheets, class newspaper, etc. ★
- Schedule field trips. ★

INSTRUCTIONAL AND SUPERVISORY★★ ASSISTANCE:

- Circulate during work time to answer questions.
- Play learning games with students.
- Help students who have been absent catch up.
- Supervise students in learning centers.
- Show pupils how to use games and equipment.
- Help students read directions.
- Supervise pupil cleanup of work area.
- Supervise students in cafeteria, bus area or playground.
- Supervise games during indoor recess.
- Help young children with coats, sweaters, etc.

- Assist teacher during field trips.
- Supervise one group while teacher is busy with another group.
- Assist substitute teacher.
- Talk to students.
- Listen to students.
- Help resolve student conflicts.
- Read to a child, small group or class.
- Listen to a child read.
- Help students make tape recordings.
- Write assignments on the chalkboard.
- Conduct drill activities with individual students or small groups.

★ Can be done at home.
★★ Supervision of students is the legal responsibility of the teacher as a school district employee. Check with your school administrator about the permissibility of leaving your students with another adult.

Student helpers and teacher aides

How Students Can Help

Expect student assistance to help make your classroom an optimum learning environment. What happens in class is a responsibility which should be shared among students, their parents, the school and the teacher.

Consider making a list of jobs for students to do. Set aside a short period at the end of each week for a class cleanup. Play music that your students will enjoy. Tell students they may talk, but the noise level must be low enough so they can hear the record.

Ideas for your student job list.

Take a look at the Chores Chart on page 23.

- Pass out papers.
- Sort paper.
- Collate and staple packets.
- Water plants.
- Wipe counter tops, desk tops, windowsills and chalk ledges.
- Dust.
- Straighten classroom library.
- Return books to school library.
- Sharpen pencils.
- Pass out materials.
- Clean cage of classroom pet.

Students Please cut animal pictures from magazines and put in box Thanks!

Handy sign holder—
Nail two spring clothespins to the wall. Works great—costs pennies! Easy to change the sign!

Set up a self-help center in your classroom. Your students can help you prepare assignments during free time or indoor recess.

FS-8302 Instant Idea Book

Sharing responsibility with students

Students Can Help!

Encourage students to share responsibility for classroom activities. It will develop their personal autonomy and lighten your workload too!

• When one student is absent, appoint another student to be responsible for collecting work and writing down assignments for the absent student. Tell this student to make a construction-paper folder for the absent student. Leaving the folder on the student's desk will remind him or her to collect work for the absentee.

• Students can be responsible for recording attendance and/or lunch buyers. Try several different methods until you find the one that works best for you. Students will develop a sense of responsibility and you will save lots of time.

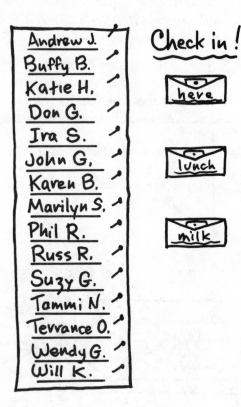

Post a class list on your bulletin board. Every morning, students hang tags next to their names to indicate attendance, lunch and milk. Absentees can be spotted quickly. Teacher can tally or appoint a classroom monitor.

Make tags in different colors for easy tallying.

Punch hole for hanging tags on pins.

Appoint a student to remove tags at the end of each school day.

Sharing responsibility with students

Another Easy Attendance Idea

Make 3" × 5" cards by pasting together a piece of green construction paper and a piece of red construction paper. Make enough cards for each student.

Put a card in each pocket, red side showing. As students enter the classroom in the morning, they turn their cards to green to indicate attendance.

Appoint an attendance monitor who will turn all cards back to red at the end of each school day.

Write student names on pockets or number 1-30 as shown. (See page 22 for information about using a number system.)

• Insist that students put finished work in the workbasket, right-side-up with their names at the top.

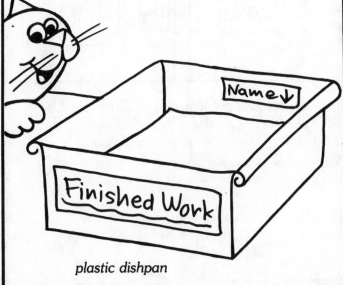

plastic dishpan

• Set out several labeled workbaskets so work is sorted for you.
Use a clothespin to hold labels.

Sharing responsibility with students

- Appoint a paper monitor to collect completed work from students. The paper monitor must make sure that all papers have been turned in and that each paper has the student's name on it before putting work in the workbasket.

- Set up a supply table where students can get materials (writing paper, pencils, erasers, crayons, scissors, etc.). Keep the supply table in the same location all year.

Ask students to let you know when supplies are running low!

- Establish a place where you post important information for students, aides and substitutes. Post bus schedules, emergency procedures, class schedule, etc.

- Write the names of your students **three times** on a blank duplicating master. Duplicate and cut into three strips. As students place completed assignments in the workbasket, they must check off their names on the class list strip. (Tape the strip next to the workbasket.) Paper clip worksheets together with the class list on top. As you correct the papers, you can write the grades on the class list. Then, use the class list strip to record grades in your grade book.

See page 17 for a reproducible class list!

FS-8302 Instant Idea Book

Names	✓	Grade	Names	✓	Grade	Names	✓	Grade

Duplicate, cut into 3 strips.

©Frank Schaffer Publications, Inc.

FS-8302 Instant Idea Book

Helping students get organized

Work Folders

Make student work folders. For example, give each student a reading folder at the beginning of the reading period. If you have three reading groups, you can name each group and make folders in three different colors. This speeds up the sorting and passing out process. At the end of the period, students put completed work in their folders and pass them in. If a student forgets to put his or her name on a paper, you know whose paper it is because the folder has the student's name written on the front. A reading folder could also contain a progress record for reading kits or a list of activities that each child has completed as well as a reading contract or assignment sheet. (See ideas for contracts on page 55.)

How to make four different folders:

① Four-Pocket Folder

(made from two pieces of 12″ × 18″ construction paper)
Each pocket can hold 8½″ × 11″ papers if stapled along the edges.

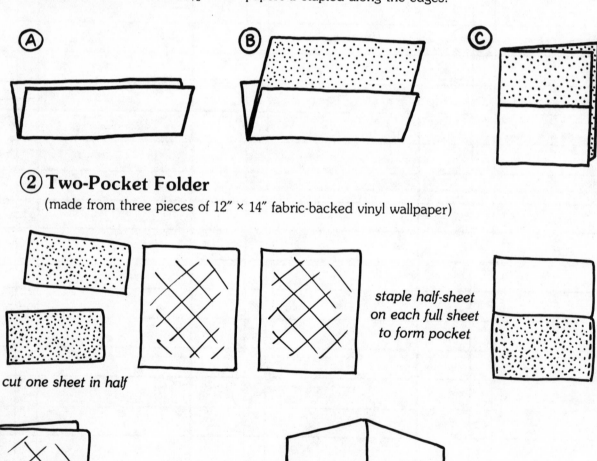

② Two-Pocket Folder

(made from three pieces of 12″ × 14″ fabric-backed vinyl wallpaper)

staple half-sheet on each full sheet to form pocket

cut one sheet in half

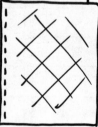

outside view of folder

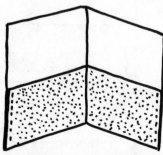

inside view of folder

③ **One-Pocket Folder**

(made from one 12″ × 18″ piece of construction paper)
The pocket holds half-sheets of paper or activity cards.

 ④ **Student-Made Work Folder**

(made from one piece of 12″ × 18″ paper)

Fold paper in half (as shown) to make a folder. Students write their names on the front and decorate their folder to match the appropriate unit of study.

Students keep work-in-progress in the folder. When finished with the unit, completed work is stapled inside the folder, graded and taken home.

It's a good idea to pass out folders at the beginning of the work period and collect them at the end. Otherwise they tend to get destroyed in student's desks.

12″ × 18″ construction paper folded once

• Leave an extra stapler near the classroom door. Students can staple their loose papers together as they leave. (Use a shoelace to tie the stapler to a cupboard handle near the door so it won't "walk away.")

Helping students get organized

Name Tags

Put a name tag on each desk at the beginning of the school year. Name tags are helpful when you are passing out folders or graded papers.

Use clear contact paper to cover name tags on desk tops so they last all year!

Left or Right?

Place right/left signs on the front wall of your classroom, above the right and left corners of your chalkboard. Some teachers put right/left signs on all four walls!

Book Drop

Place a Book Drop box near the classroom door. Students can put school library books in the box instead of in their desks—soon to be forgotten!

Take-Home Briefcase

Make a take-home briefcase for each student. Fold a piece of tagboard. Staple the sides, write each student's name and room number on the front and laminate (optional). Students use their briefcases for taking work home on Fridays. Briefcases are brought back to school on Monday and reused each week.

Use a storage box for briefcases—they get crumpled in desks!

Helping students get organized

Hang signs to:

- give directions,
- indicate specific areas in the class-room and
- post announcements.

Attach a paper clip to each end of a strand of yarn. Insert one paper clip in the edge of a ceiling tile or light fixture. Fasten a sign on the other paper clip. Signs are easy to change—simply attach a new one to the paper clip. When you don't need a sign in that area, let the "sign hanger" dangle.

Did you check the coatrack? lunch shelf? mail box? ☺

Science Center

Listening Center
① Check off your name on the list
② Put on head phones
③ Insert tape
④ Press green button ●○

*Save **all** signs for reuse!*

Cardboard Clipboards

Have a stack of clipboards available for students to use as a firm writing surface when they are away from their desks (in the reading circle, on field trips, etc.).

Easy to make: 9″ × 12″ cardboard rectangle with two clothespins to hold paper in place.

Shoe Box Desk Drawer

Give students shoe boxes to keep inside their desks. Students may bring boxes from home or ask a shoe store manager to save them for you!

A shoe box desk drawer gives students a place to keep small items (lunch money, pencils, scissors, etc.). Eliminates searching through desks to find small items. Students just pull out their "desk drawer."

FS-8302 Instant Idea Book

Helping students get organized

What's Your Number?

Use a number system to help organize your classroom and save time. Number student names in your grade book. Tell each student what his or her number is. You may want to write the numbers on name tags to help students remember. Calling them Secret Agent Numbers adds a sense of mystery. Take a look at the following list of ideas for using the number system:

- Have students write their numbers on the upper right-hand corner of all assignments. Papers can be arranged in numerical order for quick recording in your grade book. When you arrange papers in numerical order, it is easy to spot those that are missing.

- Have students line up in numerical order. This will end complaints about students "taking cuts" or being first in line. Simply call out the number of the first person in line. Say "Line up starting with number 18," and your students will line up 18 to 30 and 1 to 17. During fire drills, it helps to have students line up in numerical order—you can quickly make sure that everyone is in line.

- Give each student a spring-type clothespin with his or her number on it. If you are doing an art project which involves many pieces and will take several days to complete, tell students to clip their pieces together with the clothespin and place them in a box. Passing out materials the following day is easy; everyone receives a complete set of pieces for their projects.

- Students can clip their clothespins to wipe-away cards or matching activities that need to be corrected by the teacher.

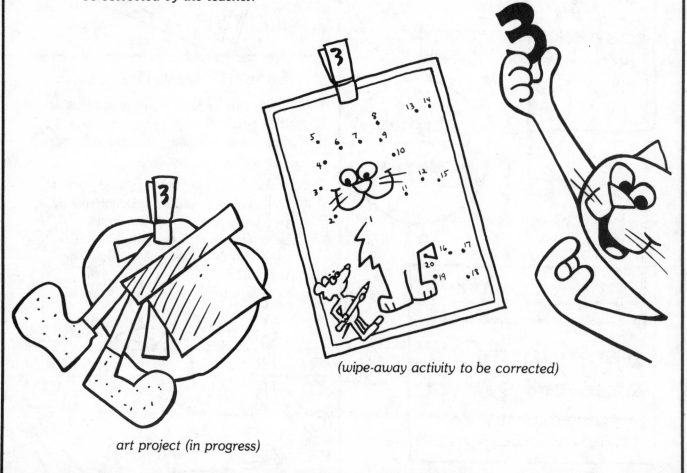

(wipe-away activity to be corrected)

art project (in progress)

Helping students get organized

- Number a set of mailboxes from 1 to 30. Instead of collecting papers, have students "mail" their paper to you by putting them in their mailboxes. You can tell at a glance if all the papers have been handed in. Your paper monitor will collect the papers in numerical order, clip them together and put them in the finished workbasket.

- Number popsicle sticks from 1 to 30 and put them in a coffee can. When you need a child to do something, pick a number. This ends complaints about favoritism.

- Make sure you call on every student every day by picking numbers from the coffee can. Pick a number and call on that student but do not replace his or her number in the can. Continue to pick numbers throughout the school day. You will call on a different student each time! (You will quickly learn the names that correspond to the numbers, so when you draw a number you can say the student's name instead of the number.)

- Use numbers to select groups of students quickly. For example, you can have students 1 through 5 do Current Events Reports on Monday, students 6 through 10 on Tuesday, etc.

- Make a Chores Chart numbered 1 to 30. Rotate chore cards on a weekly basis.

3" × 5" cards

Numbers are reusable from year to year.

FS-8302 Instant Idea Book

Parent Communication Counts!

Make meetings with parents more valuable by improving your communication skills. It's easy to earn an A+ with parents when you follow these tips for success. A list of ideas for parents to help their children learn is also included. You'll be eager to try these suggestions for parent communication. Soon, you'll be an expert in the art of public relations. And parents will be well-informed about their children's lives at school.

When parents come to school. . .

Open House—Make It a Super-Duper Success!

A visit to your classroom can be a very special and enjoyable experience!

- **Sign In, Please. . .**
  Have a "guest book" for parents to sign. Staple lined paper inside a construction paper or wallpaper cover to make your guest book.

- **Display Work from Each Child**
  Post a sample of good work completed by each student in your class.

- **Display and Label Materials**
  Put texts and workbooks out for parents to peruse.

- **Parent Notes**
  Tell each student to write a welcome note to his or her parent(s). Leave the notes in student mailboxes or on their desks for parents to read.

- **Visitor's Guide**
  Give each parent a list of things to see in your classroom.★

- **Duplicate Important Information**
  Give parents a copy of the class schedule, class or school rules and a list of items their child should bring to school.★★

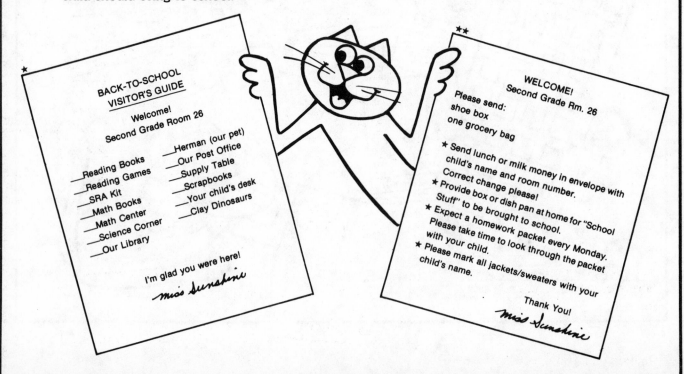

When parents come to school. . .

- ## Make a Welcome Banner to Hang On or Near the Door:

  Use a 5′ or 6′ × 36″ length of butcher paper—dark-colored paper is excellent for banners!

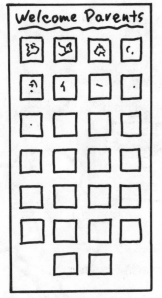

Each student draws a picture of his or her family. Pictures are pasted on the banner.

Each student draws a self-portrait, cuts it out and pastes it on the banner. Write student names under each "face."

(handprints)

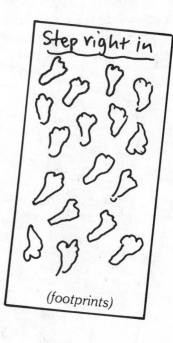

(footprints)

Students trace their handprint (or footprint) on colored construction paper. Cut and paste on banner.

Include your handprint too!

Effective parent conferences

Parent conferences provide an opportunity for parents and teachers to share information and ideas with the goal of improving the student's learning experience. Use the following list of tips and techniques to help improve the quality of your meetings with parents.

- Schedule parent conferences carefully. Do not schedule too many conferences in one day, especially with parents of students who are doing poorly.

- To make your conference schedule less hectic, consider holding a few conferences the week before, or the week after, the official parent-conference week. Obtain administrative approval first, if necessary.

- Make sure your parent-conference schedule is convenient for working parents.

- Give parents a survey form★ to fill out and bring to the conference. This helps the parent focus on his or her child and formulate questions before the conference.

★

Dear _____,

I am always looking for ways to improve our communication. Please answer the following questions and bring this form to our conference on _____.

Miss Sunshine

1. How does your child feel about school?
   _____
2. Does your child talk about school? _____
3. What does your child like best about school?
   _____
4. What does your child like least about school?
   _____
5. What do you think is your child's strongest subject? _____
6. What do you think is your child's weakest subject? _____
7. Other information or questions: _____
   _____

FS-8302 Instant Idea Book

Effective parent conferences. . .

- Put a few chairs in the hall so parents can be comfortable while they wait for their conference. Leave a few magazines out there too!

- Post your daily conference schedule on the door. Stay on schedule. If a parent arrives late and it will throw off your schedule, reschedule the conference. If you want to schedule a break for yourself, write it on the schedule as a "meeting" and go relax during that break.

Post schedule in waiting area. →

Go to the office, relax, take a break. →

Tells parents whether or not they are in the right place. →

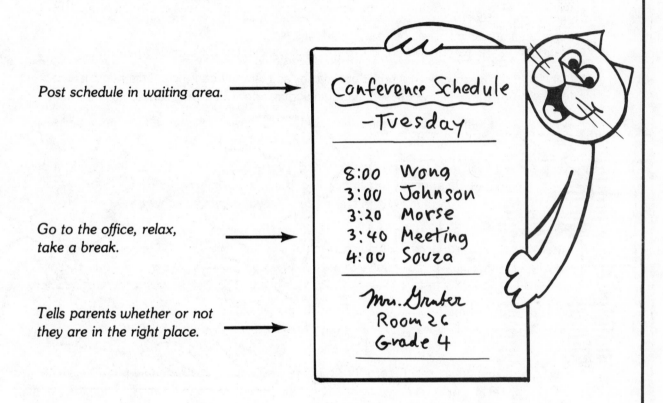

Conference Schedule
— Tuesday

8:00 Wong
3:00 Johnson
3:20 Morse
3:40 Meeting
4:00 Souza

Mrs. Gruber
Room 26
Grade 4

- Conduct conferences at a table instead of from behind your desk. (This will be more informal and, therefore, less threatening to parents.) Provide note paper and pens so parents can write down information. Keep note paper handy for writing down information you want to remember too. Make sure you have enough adult-size chairs for everyone at the conference.

- Stay on the subject. If the parent digresses, it is your responsibility to get the conference back on track.

- If you do not understand what a parent means, paraphrase what he or she has said and then ask the parent if you are correct. If you are not sure of what a parent is saying, try to clarify the parent's statement by saying,
  "Can you give me an example?"
  "I'm not sure what you mean."
  "Is this what you are saying?" (Paraphrase what was said.)
  "I'm having a problem understanding exactly what you mean."

Effective parent conferences. . .

- If a conference does not go smoothly, schedule another meeting with the parent or parents. You may want to ask the principal to attend this second conference.

- If you or the parent brings up a subject such as retention or special testing procedures, make a note of this on the conference form before the parent signs it. Then you will have a written record showing that the subject was discussed at the conference. For example, you can write: "retention was discussed," "psychological testing was discussed," "transfer to another classroom was discussed," etc. Noting this information is helpful to you, to the parent and to next year's teacher, who will read your notes on the carbon copy of the conference form which will be in the student's file.

- Student records are available to parents as legislated in the Family Rights and Privacy Act of 1974. If parents want to see school records or add information to records, refer them to your administrator. He or she will make sure that prescribed procedures are followed.

- Write a list of things parents can do to help their children at home. Duplicate your list and give it to parents during the conference. (see page 33 for ideas.)

- Keep parents informed throughout the school year—use the techniques described on pages 34-43. When parents know what's happening at school, conferences can be more productive. Well informed parents tend to feel more positive about the school too.

- Be cautious about suggesting specific tutors, learning clinics, family counseling centers or other professional services. Instead, you might ask the parent, "if he or she has considered seeking outside help for the child such as . . ." Recommendation of a specific outside service could make the school district responsible, especially if that service proves to be unsatisfactory.

- Keep a record of the parents you have conferences with in your plan book or on your calendar. Also, write down any phone calls or incidental, at-the-door conferences you have with parents.

- Start keeping an anecdotal record for students who have serious behavioral or learning problems. This record will come in handy during parent meetings, when writing special help requests for these students and for explaining the problems to a school nurse, counselor or administrator.

- Don't compare one child to another.

- Avoid educational jargon. Use language that parents understand.

- Try to see things from the parents' point of view.

- Be sure parents know that you care and that you have a sincere interest in their child's personal and educational growth.

- End the conference on a positive note.

FS-8302 Instant Idea Book

Communicate Clearly on Report Cards and Conference Forms

Make a list of words and phrases to use on parent conference forms, report cards and notes to parents. Add your own ideas to the following list of suggested comments.

Positive Comments:

- off to a good start
- confident
- high level or self-esteem
- eager to please
- wants to do well
- grasps new concepts quickly
- willing to work hard·
- has many friends
- responds well to praise and/or constructive criticism
- accepts responsibility
- sets high standards
- self-motivated
- self-starter
- is a leader

- at top of group
- at top of class
- doing well in all academic subjects
- having a good year
- takes pride in work
- enthusiastic
- high interest level
- all-around good student
- cooperative
- creative
- especially talented in . . .
- working at grade level
- pleased with progress
- mature

Not-So-Positive Comments:

- inattentive
- overactive
- fine motor difficulties
- gross motor difficulties
- slow completing work
- does not complete work
- hard to discipline
- short attention span
- has difficulty verbalizing
- has difficulty concentrating
- unpredictable
- defiant
- impatient
- overly sensitive
- has difficulty following oral directions
- has difficulty following written directions
- has difficulty with (subject)
- has difficulty accepting responsibility
- has difficulty organizing and planning work
- tends to daydream

- teases other children
- easily frustrated
- has difficulty keeping up with group
- disturbs others
- has difficulty working independently
- demands too much attention
- easily distracted by others
- talking interferes with work
- unable to maintain friendships
- seems unsure of self
- resorts to show-off behavior
- has difficulty concentrating on schoolwork
- has not developed problem-solving skills
- depends on rote learning
- poor work habits hinder progress
- began the year slowly
- displays lack of interest
- displays lack of motivation
- dependent behavior
- easily influenced by peers

How parents can help

Help Parents Provide Learning Experiences at Home!

Consider setting up a parent resource library in your classroom or at your school. Books, flash cards, games and learning activities could be available for parents to check out and use with their children at home.

Give parents guidelines for working with students. Suggest that parent:

- set aside a regular time to work with the child.

- keep the time period short. (Give parents a suggested length of time—some may think an hour is a short time period for a young child.)

- work on one concept at a time.

- reward progress to make the learning experience fun.

You can give parents these guidelines for working with their child during parent conferences or at open house. Duplicate a form for parents to jot down the ideas, they are more likely to actually do them!

Second Grade
Mrs. Gruber
Working with your child:
1.
2.
3.
4.
Ten activities:
1.
2.   6.
3.   7.
4.   8.
5.   9.
            10.

Parents appreciate receiving specific suggestions about how to help their child learn. You can communicate ideas to parents via:

- parent conferences.

- parent notes and newsletters.

- open house gatherings.

- parent handbook or guide prepared by the school.

- duplicate a copy of page 33 for parents.

How parents can help

Check this list of things parents can do to help their children learn:

- Read to your child.
- Listen to your child read.
- Play games with your child.
- Help your child get a library card from the public library nearest you. Encourage your child to go to the library as often as possible.
- Go to the library with your child. Help him or her pick out interesting books to read.
- Find out about activities for children that take place at your library.
- Talk to your child about subjects that are interesting to him or her.
- Listen to your child.
- Set aside a special "reading time." Let your child know that you look forward to and enjoy your time together.
- Give your child his or her own place to keep books.
- Write notes to your child.
- Help your child write letters and notes.
- Encourage your child to keep a scrapbook about a subject that interests him or her: stamps, dogs, birds, trucks, etc.
- Limit your child's television watching—select certain shows to watch. Turn the television set on for the show and turn it off immediately after the show is over.
- Read and discuss your child's schoolwork.
- Provide materials such as crayons, art paper and paints for creative projects.
- Give your child a calendar so he or she can write down special events and mark off each day.
- Help your child make a telephone directory with the names and phone numbers of his or her friends.
- Ask your child to add a sentence or two to letters you write to far-away relatives. (Young children can dictate a sentence for you to write.)
- Give your child specific duties to perform on a regular basis at home.
- Let your child help you prepare dinner.
- Subscribe to a children's magazine (in the child's name).
- Bring books for your child to read in the car while he or she waits for you to run errands.
- Look up words in the dictionary with your child.
- Encourage your child to start a collection of rocks, stamps, etc.
- Encourage your child to show his or her schoolwork to your relatives and friends.
- When traveling, read road signs with your child. Discuss what they mean.
- Show your child how to use a yardstick, ruler and tape measure for measuring objects around the house.
- Provide counting experiences for your child.
- Show your child how to count change.
- Give your child a special place (box, dish pan, etc.) to keep items he or she must take to school each morning. (This ends last-minute searching for library books, papers, bike keys, etc., all of which can cause your child to be late for school.)
- Show your child how to tell time.

Communicating with parents

Keep Parents Informed About What's Happening at School!

Parents want to be informed. The more they feel "in touch" with what's happening in their child's classroom, the better they feel about their child's overall learning experience.

Become a public relations expert! Good public relations can be planned; bad public relations just happens. Here are some tips to help you become a PR expert:

Weekly Work Packets: Give each child a weekly packet of work to take home. Tell parents which day of the week the packet will be sent home. Some teachers like to send work home on Mondays instead of at the end of the week. Parents might pay more attention to their child's work at the beginning of the school week than at the beginning of the weekend. (See page 20 for ideas about making a student briefcase for carrying school-work home.)

Weekly Work Forms: Send home a "Sign-and-return" form with each child's weekly work packet so you know whether or not parents have seen the student's work. (See reproducible form on page 39.)

Sample Alphabet: Duplicate and send home a sample alphabet for each parent. Parents will have a sample of the manuscript or cursive writing style that their child is using at school.

Weekly Progress Reports: Send home a weekly progress report for some or all of the students in your class. (See reproducible form on page 39.)

Save time by signing forms before duplicating. They will be pre-signed and ready-to-use!

 FS-8302 Instant Idea Book

Communicating with parents

Daily Progress Reports: Send home a daily progress report for students who need a plan for behavior control. (See reproducible form on page 40.)

(See reproducible form on page 40.)

Daily Progress Report

❀ ❀ ❀ _____ (date)

For: _____
(student)

From: _____
(teacher)

Morning: _____

Recess: _____

Lunch: _____

Afternoon: _____

Other: _____

Please sign—have your child bring this note back to school tomorrow.

_____
(parent signature)

Home Reading Log: Give each child a home reading log to keep track of reading at home. You may want to award a "prize" when a certain number of minutes has been recorded. See the list of no-cost rewards on page 61. A reproducible home reading log is provided on page 39.

Home Reading Log

Week of _____

Day	Minutes	Read To
Mon.		
Tues.		
Wed.		
Thurs.		
Fri.		
Sat.		
Sun.		

Student _____

Parent _____

Teacher _____

Weekly Newsletters: Send home a weekly newsletter. You can prepare the newsletter during the school day. Parents will enjoy receiving it—you can include the newsletter in the student's weekly work packet. Tell each child to make a folder for storing the newsletters at home. Offer a "prize" at the end of the school year for students who have a copy of each newsletter in their folders. Students can reread their newsletter collections as well as share them with friends and relatives.

Put a copy of the newsletter in your principal's mailbox each week!

FS-8302 Instant Idea Book

How to Write a Weekly Newletter during School Time

- *Kindergarten, First, Second Grades:*
Duplicate the newsletter format on page 42. At the end of each school day, ask your students for information to put in the newsletter. Elicit ideas from the class about what happened at school that day. Write this information in appropriate section of the newsletter. On Fridays, fill in the newletter just before lunch so you can duplicate it and send it home with the end-of-the-week work packets.

- *Second, Third, Fourth Grades:*
Duplicate the newsletter format and give each student a copy. Elicit ideas from the class. Write sentences on the chalkboard and have students copy the information on their newsletter. (Use the newsletter format on page 42.)

- *Third through Sixth Grades:*
Instead of doing the newsletter every day, make it a letter-writing activity at the end of the week. On Fridays, ask students to call out ideas for the letter. Write this information on the chalkboard, using a letter format. (See illustration) Students will copy the letter as a penmanship exercise. While you are writing information on the chalkboard, explain the letter format and point out rules for capitalization and punctuation. Students must show you their letters before taking them home.

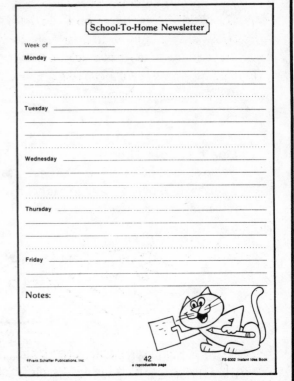

School-To-Home Newsletter

Week of _____
Monday _____
Tuesday
Wednesday
Thursday
Friday
Notes:

©Frank Schaffer Publications, Inc.   42
a reproducible page   FS-8302 Instant Idea Book

January 15, 1983

Dear Parents,
    This week at school was very busy. We started a new social studies unit on California history. I can make a model of a mission for extra credit.
    We are making books for first-grade students. The books explain rules for bicycle safety.
    Mrs. Gruber is reading us a book called **Trumpet of The Swan** by E.B. White.
        Sincerely,

Communicating with parents

• *Fourth, Fifth and Sixth Grades:*
On Fridays, ask students what happened at school that week. List their responses on the chalkboard. Tell your students to write a letter to their parents which includes at least five events from the list. Evaluate the letters for neatness and accuracy before students take them home.

Ideas for parents letter
- field trip
- science experiment
- PE activity
- oral report
- made new scrapbook
- our clay is in the kiln
- new student in class
  Jonathon Cunningham

Scrapbooks: Students staple construction paper or wallpaper pages together to make scrapbooks. Each week, students will put samples of their work in the scrapbooks. When scrapbooks are full, students can take them home and start new ones.

Homework: Use a homework form every week. Write homework assignments on the chalkboard for students to copy each day. The form becomes a record of completed work and provides a place for parents to sign. Use the reproducible homework form on **page 41.**

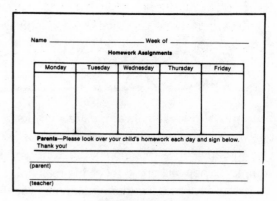

| Name | Week of |
| Homework Assignments |

Monday	Tuesday	Wednesday	Thursday	Friday

Parents—Please look over your child's homework each day and sign below. Thank you!

(parent)

(teacher)

Work to Do: Send home incomplete work to be finished and returned to school. (Use the form on page 40.) Keep a record of papers you have sent home. Remember to verify completion.

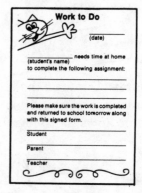

Work to Do
(date)

_____ needs time at home
(student's name)
to complete the following assignment:

Please make sure the work is completed and returned to school tomorrow along with this signed form.

Student

Parent

Teacher

Duplicate parent communication forms so they will always be handy and ready to use! Sign your name on the forms before duplicating—saves time!

FS-8302 Instant Idea Book

Communicating with parents

Basal Readers: Encourage students to take basal readers home so they can read to their parents or siblings. Allowing students to demonstrate their successes is very important. A form letter for sending basal reders home is on page 40.

Basal Reader

(date)

Dear Parent,
   Your child wants to read a story to you from our basal reader.
   Please return the book _____
_____

   You'll enjoy hearing your child read.
Thank you for helping—it does make a difference!
Sincerely,

(teacher)

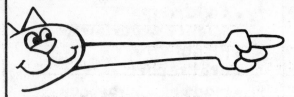

Please Help: Let parents know when their child needs extra practice. A reproducible parent note is on page 39.

Please Help!

(date)

Dear Parent,
_____ will benefit from
(student)
extra practice at home on
_____
_____

_____ (teacher)

Please sign—your child should bring this note back to school.

_____
(parent)

Flashcards: Use the mini-flashcard format on page 43 to make take-home flashcards for math or reading practice. Write math problems or vocabulary words on the form, reproduce it and give a copy to each student. Or, give copies of the blank flashcards to students and tell them to write spelling words, reading vocabulary or math problems. Students can take their mini-flashcards home for practice and review.

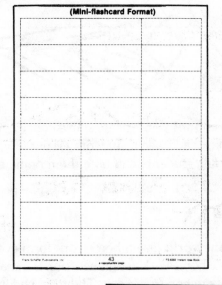

(Mini-flashcard Format)

43

Summer Review Program: A few weeks before the school year ends, ask parents to send six self-addressed, stamped envelopes to school for their child. Use the envelopes to send six different worksheets to students during the summer. They will enjoy receiving mail and the worksheets will provide important skill practice during summer vacation. Use the summer review parent letter on page 40.

Summer Review Program

(date)

   All Students can benefit from reviewing school work during summer vacation. Therefore, I want to mail worksheets to your child during the summer recess. Please look over the completed worksheets with your child.
   Please send six stamped envelopes addressed to your child to school. I will use the envelopes to mail worksheets to your child. Everyone enjoys receiving mail and your child will get valuable practice.
   Thank you for helping—it does make a difference!
Sincerely,

(teacher)

Parent Notes: Duplicate the note paper format on page 41 so you can write notes to parents.

A note from teacher to parent—

To: _____ From: _____ Date: _____
_____
_____
_____
_____
_____

FS-8302 Instant Idea Book

Weekly Work

Attached is your child's schoolwork from this week.

Please look through the packet with your child.

Sign this form and send it back to school.

Thank you.

_____ _____
(teacher's signature)   (date)

_____ _____
(parent's signature)   (date)

_____
(student's name)

Weekly Progress Report

For: _____
         (student)

From: _____
          (teacher)

Date: _____

Subject	Work	Behavior
Reading		
Language Arts		
Math		
Other: _____		

Comments: _____
_____

Sign and return: _____

Please Help!

_____
(date)

Dear Parent,

_____ will benefit from
(student)

extra practice at home on

_____

_____

_____
          (teacher)

Please sign. Your child should bring this note back to school.

_____
(parent)

Home Reading Log

Week of _____

Day	Minutes	Read To
Mon.		
Tues.		
Wed.		
Thurs.		
Fri.		
Sat.		
Sun.		

Student _____

Parent _____

Teacher _____

Daily Progress Report

✿ ✿ ✿ _____
(date)

For: _____
(student)

From: _____
(teacher)

_____

Morning: _____

Recess: _____

Lunch: _____

Afternoon: _____

Other: _____

Please sign. Have your child bring this note back to school tomorrow.

_____
(parent signature)

Work to Do

_____
(date)

_____ needs time at home
(student's name)
to complete the following assignment:

_____

_____

_____

Please make sure the work is completed and returned to school tomorrow along with this signed form.

_____
Student

_____
Parent

_____
Teacher

Summer Review Program

_____
(date)

Dear Parents,

All students can benefit from reviewing school work during summer vacation. Therefore, I want to mail worksheets to your child during the summer recess. Please look over the completed worksheets with your child.

Please send six stamped envelopes addressed to your child to school. I will use the envelopes to mail worksheets to your child. Everyone enjoys receiving mail and your child will get valuable practice.

Thank you for helping. It does make a difference!

Sincerely,

_____
(teacher)

Basal Reader

_____
(date)

Dear Parent,

Your child wants to read a story to you from our basal reader.

Please return the book _____

_____

You'll enjoy hearing your child read. Thank you for helping. It does make a difference!

Sincerely,

_____
(teacher)

A note from teacher to parent—

To: _____ From: _____ Date: _____

_____

_____

_____

_____

_____

_____

_____

_____

- -

Name _____ Week of _____

Homework Assignments

Monday	Tuesday	Wednesday	Thursday	Friday

Parents—Please look over your child's homework each day and sign below.
Thank you!

_____

(parent)

_____

(teacher)

School-To-Home Newsletter

Week of _____

Monday _____

_____

_____

· ·

Tuesday _____

_____

_____

· ·

Wednesday _____

_____

_____

· ·

Thursday _____

_____

_____

· ·

Friday _____

_____

_____

Notes:

(Mini-flashcard Format)

FS-8302 Instant Idea Book

 **My ideas for parent communication. . .**

FS-8302 Instant Idea Book

Classroom Management Tactics That Really Work!

Learn how to improve student work habits and increase class participation. When students are actively involved, they learn more!

Classroom-tested strategies are included for ensuring good behavior from individual students as well as from your entire class. A list of no-cost rewards for students is provided along with self-enhancing techniques for classroom management.

Improving student work habits

How to Give Directions Effectively:

Many students do not pay attention when directions are given because they plan to ask for individual help from the teacher. Every class has a few students who are overly-dependent on the teacher for individual help. This problem can be solved by giving directions very carefully and by spelling out specific procedures for students who need individual help.

1) Insist that students sit in a prescribed manner when you are giving directions. For example, you might require that desks be cleared, hands on desk tops and all students looking directly at you. Indicate that you are ready to give directions and want complete attention by saying, "Time to listen!"

2) Do not permit students to begin working until you say, "Time to start!" When students start working while you are giving directions, they miss important information.

3) Tell students that you will **NOT** answer questions during the first five minutes of the work period. Set a timer for five minutes when students begin working and do not answer any questions during that period. When students know that you are not available for a private tutorial session, they will listen to the directions carefully.

4) Write directions step-by-step on the chalkboard. Number them in sequence.

5) Read all directions to the class. Point to each direction on the chalkboard as you read it.

6) Do an example with your class.

7) Tell students when to begin working; remind them about the five-minute, no-question period. (See idea 3 above.)

8) Tell students where to put finished work.

9) Tell students what to do after they have finished the assignment.

Establish Procedures for Students Who Need Teacher Assistance:

Valuable time is wasted when students have to wait for help from the teacher. Try the following tips to keep lost time to a minimum and effectively assist students.

Teach new skills to the entire class. Put students who need help in a small group; then re-teach the skills.

1) Train students to do as much work as they can on a work sheet **before** asking for help. Students should skip problems they cannot do. When the worksheet (or workbook page) has been completed, they must go back to the problems they could not do and try them again. Only after a second attempt can they ask for help from the teacher.

2) Establish procedures for getting individual help:

- **Take a Number** (like at the butcher shop).

- **Flag on Name Tag** (like on mailboxes). Student raises the flag when help is needed.

- **Question Chair** for student to sit in. Student waits for help from the teacher.

Make an OPEN/CLOSED sign. When the sign says CLOSED, you are not available to answer any questions.

FS-8302 Instant Idea Book

Improving student work habits

• I Need Help!

3) Establish an area on the chalkboard where students write their names and the page number(s) or problem number(s) with which they need help. The teacher helps students in order, but if several students need help on the same problem, they can be helped as a group. Saves time for the teacher and students.

> ## I need help!
> | Name | Problem Number |
> |------|----------------|
> | Kim | _____ 11 |
> | Sara | _____ 5 |
> | Mark | _____ 11,12 |
> | David | _____ 10 |

(You can help Kim and Mark together on problem 11.)

Use Symbols to Tell Students What to Do!

 work with a partner
Put on file folder games or other partner activities.

 parent
Use on forms needing parent signatures.

 self-check
Students may self-correct that activity or assignment.

 required work

 teacher
   • *If you have an envelope of your materials in the back of a kit used by students, mark it with a* .

• *When you help a student and plan to check on his or her progress later, skip ahead on the worksheet and write a* Ⓣ *symbol. When the student reaches that point, he or she must check back with the teacher:*

• *If you want students to show you their work at a certain point, include a teacher checkpoint when writing directions on the chalkboard.*

> Do problems 1-10.
> Ⓣ
> Do problems 11-15.
> Put work in basket.
> Read library book.

• *Use* Ⓣ *on contracts to indicate the place where you will write the grade or check mark to show that the work has been completed (as shown on page 55).*

Improving student work habits

Vary the Pace to Maintain High Productivity Levels!

- Follow an individual activity with a group activity.

- Follow a quiet, "sit-in-your-chair" activity with something that involves movement and discussion.

- Instead of a 30-minute work period, let students work for 15 minutes, then take a 5-minute break. They may stand up, get a drink, talk quietly or sharpen a pencil. Then have another 10 minutes of work time. Students will produce more during a timed period that has a break.

- Reduce the amount of time you normally allow for an assignment. Tell students that you will set a timer and you want them to work as quickly as they can until the bell rings. Timing tasks results in on-task behavior and higher productivity.

- Before students begin a worksheet, ask them to put a "green light" on the place where thay are ready to start. Ask them to pick the spot where they expect to be in five minutes and mark it with a "red light." (Lights are simply dots made with a green or red crayon.) Then set a timer for five minutes and say "Go." When the timer rings, ask students if they reached the red light. Goal setting increases productivity!

- Write a behavior code on the chalkboard. Use codes to show students which kind of behavior is expected during a particular period.
  For example:

  NT = No Talking
  SSS = Stand, Stretch & Sit
  CU = Clean Up
  TT = Talking Time

- Use a traffic light to signal the class about required behavior during a certain period. Use red, yellow and green construction paper circles.

How to make a traffic light:
tagboard with paper clip to hold "light"

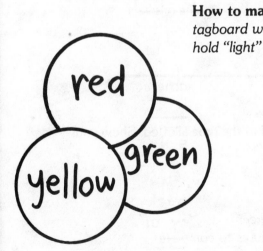

Red Light = Quiet, Sit-in-Your-Seat Work Time
Yellow Light = Work Time with Some Movement in Room
Green Light = Talking Is Permissible

Improving student work habits

- When you notice that a student is working well, touch him or her on the shoulder as you walk by the student's desk. Students are often distracted when the teacher stops to commend them verbally. But if you walk by and just touch the student, he or she will keep right on working!

- Have privacy screens available for students who are easily distracted. Privacy screens can be made from three sides of a cardboard box. Let students help themselves to screens.

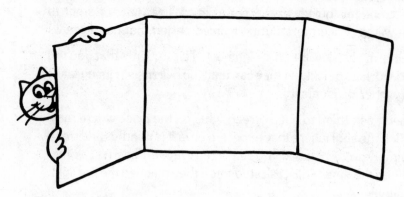

privacy screen (folds flat for storage)

- Establish a Quiet Zone in the classroom. When students work in that area, no talking is permitted. Post a sign: Quiet Zone—No Talking Please!

- Let students wear headsets to screen out noise. This can help talkative students keep quiet.

Shhh...
Quiet Zone

- Divide an assignment into sections so it can be completed in the time allotted. Show your students how to do this.

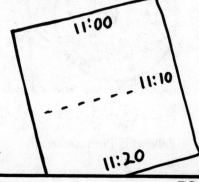

11:00

11:10

11:20

worksheet 20 minutes to complete

Students divide worksheet in sections and write time segments on the paper.

FS-8302 Instant Idea Book

A Place for Everything and Everything in Its Place

- Set a good example by keeping your classroom orderly. Insist that students keep their desks tidy. (Read the ideas for helping students become organized on pages 18-23.) Give an award to students who keep their desks neat. Periodically pick a student's name from a hat and inspect his or her desk after school. If the desk is tidy, the student earns a reward.

- Here's how to help students REALLY clean out their desks. Instead of taking everything out and stuffing it all back in their desks again, tell students to put EVERYTHING on top of their desks. Then, call out items that should be in the desks. When you call out an item (such as "one pair of scissors"), students put that item back in their desks. When you are finished calling out items, students are left with items to be taken home, discarded or put elsewhere.

See the "shoe box desk drawer" idea on page 21.

- During a period when students are working on group activities around the classroom, blink the lights on and off to indicate clean-up time. Everyone in the group must participate. When members of a group are finished with cleanup, they raise their hands and the teacher inspects to make sure materials have been put away properly. This solves the problem of students putting materials away haphazardly to be sorted out later by the teacher.

Establish a Routine to Run Your Classroom Smoothly!

When you have routine procedures, your students know what to do. That means fewer interruptions and less time wasted.

Keep unstructured time to a minimum. Develop a routine so your students know what to do as they enter the classroom.

Establish a spot on the chalkboard where you write what students should do upon entering the room. You can make a paper "picture frame" and tape it one the chalkboard or simply write "Do: _____ ." This solves the problem of students entering the room and asking, "What are we supposed to do?"

paper picture frame—tape and leave up erase and change message

Check in
Get out:
ruler
pencil
scissors

Variety Adds Interest and Fun!

Change the routine once in a while:

- Let students sit in the seats of their choice for one day or one work period.

- Switch with another teacher on your grade level and teach a lesson to his or her class.

- Teach subjects at different times of the day than usual.

Learning through participation

Actively Involve Your Students—They Will Learn More!

Make sure all students have a chance to respond, instead of just a few. Use student response cards and individual chalkboards. Participation reduces boredom and behavior problems.

Student Response Cards:

When teaching a lesson on plural endings, for example, give each student a card. Tell them to write "s" on one side of the card, and "es" on the other side. When you say a word, each student shows you the correct ending to make that word a plural. Student response cards can also be used for:

- initial consonants
- ending sounds
- vowel sounds
- counting syllables
- affixes

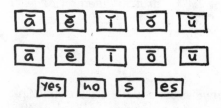

WHICH VOWEL SOUND DO YOU HEAR?

Individual Chalkboards:

Individual chalkboards can be purchased in school supply stores or you can make them. Buy a 4′ × 8′ sheet of masonite in a building supply store. Saw it into 32 squares that measure 12″ × 12″ each. (You can make larger chalkboards if you need fewer than 32.) Paint them with chalkboard paint (available in paint or building supply stores). Give each student a chalkboard and an old sock to use as an eraser. Students can keep chalk inside the socks.

Uses for chalkboards:

When teaching a lesson on plural endings, you say the word and the child writes the ending on the chalkboard and shows it to you.

When you are teaching long division or handwriting, the student writes on his or her chalkboard and you write on the board. Then the class can show you their work when you say, "Show me!"

FS-8302 Instant Idea Book

Learning through participation

Increase Student Involvement During Group Activities

- Divide your class into four or five groups. Change groups every few weeks. When the class is doing oral book reports, current events or other sharing activities, groups gather in different locations around the room. The teacher moves from group to group to monitor the activity. Each student has an opportunity to share and listen in a small group.

- Divide your class into groups by writing names on the chalkboard or by posting names on a bulletin board. Simply move the name cards around to change group members.

Move name cards to change groups!

- Increase participation in class discussions by controlling group responses. After you ask a question, say "Time to think" and count silently to five. During this five-second pause, students may not raise their hands. After counting to five, call on students. More students will want to participate in the discussion after being given time to think. The responses will reflect more thought and students will not feel as if they are in a race to see who can get their hands up first.

Self-enhancing, classroom-management ideas

Use Samples of Student Work to Teach Concepts!

Show students that you value their work by using samples to teach new concepts. Students will pay more attention to work completed by their peers than to materials prepared by the teacher.

Save stories, poems and reports written by your students. Photocopy samples of student work for use with next year's class too. For example, when you are teaching Haiku poetry, post some poems written by former students.

Make a "Group Contract"

Use a piece of tagboard to make your group contract. Clip spring-type clothespins along the side and write "Things to Do" at the top. Paste an envelope on the back of the contract. On strips of paper, write different activities that go on in your classroom. Place the paper strips in the envelope. When you want to give your students a choice of things to do, use the group contract. Simply clip the paper strips to the front of the contract. Your group contract can stand on the chalk ledge!

FS-8302 Instant Idea Book

Share Record-Keeping Responsibility with Your Students

Use contracts so students can keep track of their completed work. Giving students the opportunity to mark their own progress is motivating, self-enhancing and helps them stay organized.

Instead of writing specific assignments on contract forms, just write a general subject area. Write page numbers on the chalkboard for students to fill in on their contracts. Then the contract form can be used again. If you fill in specific assignments before duplicating the form, you will have to create new contracts daily or weekly.

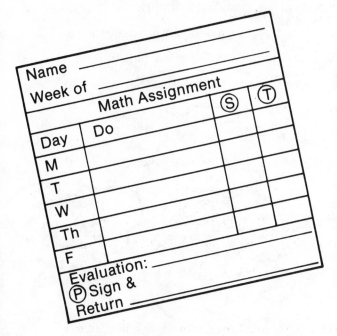

Name							
Week of							
Things to do	★	M	T	W	Th	F	Ⓣ
Basal Reader							
Workbook							
Reading Kit							
Phonics							
Reading Game							
Task Cards							
Spelling							
Language Book							
Dictionary							
Handwriting							

Ⓢ (student)　　Ⓣ (teacher)　　Ⓟ (parent)　　☆ (required work)

Let students keep track of their progress on a bar graph. Bar graphs will reinforce graphing skills, serve as progress records and are handy to show parents during parent conferences.

Give bar graphs to students along with corrected spelling tests. Collect bar graphs after students record their scores. They get destroyed when stored in student desks.

	Spelling Test Scores									
Date	Number Correct									
	1	2	3	4	5	6	7	8	9	10
October 7	▓	▓	▓	▓	▓	▓	▓			
October 14	▓	▓	▓	▓	▓	▓	▓	▓	▓	
October 21	▓	▓	▓	▓						

Self-enhancing, classroom-management ideas

Working Together Pays Off!

Find a supportive colleague to be your teaching partner.

Work with a teaching partner to reduce your work load and improve your teaching program. Here's how:

- Teach a lesson to your partner's class. If you are talented in art, teach an art lesson to both classes. Your partner will pay you back by teaching your class in his or her area of strength.

- Plan together—two heads are better than one.

- Share ideas for classroom management, timesaving and oraganization that work well for you.

- Know the routine in your partner's classroom so you can help out if he or she has a substitute.

- Be a good listener. Work out solutions to problems together with your teaching partner.

- Establish the Friday Film for Good Workers program for your two classes. (See page 57.)

- Share materials with your teaching partner.

- Share a school job (such as social chairperson, PTA representative, etc.)

- Brainstorm ideas together. You'll be amazed what fun it is to have your very own consultant!

Communicate with Every Student Every Day!

Many students demand attention and are impossible to ignore. Shy, obedient children can be easily overlooked. You can deal effectively with shy students by following these guidelines:

1. You must initiate contact.

2. Be slow, gradual and non-threatening.

3. Make statements instead of asking questions.

4. Use the walk-by-and-touch technique. (See page 50.)

5. Do not force shy children to respond.

6. Write notes to shy children.

7. Look for ways to increase their level of participation.

Classroom Management Tips:

Teachers are always looking for classroom management strategies that work! It is a good idea to use one strategy for a period of time and then switch to a different strategy. Using the same strategy for too long tends to weaken even the best of systems.

QUESTION: *How do you motivate students to finish their work?*

Friday Film for Good Workers: Reward students who work well during the week by showing a special film on Fridays. The film may be seen only by those students who have earned the privilege. Work with your teaching partner(See page 56) to implement this idea. One teacher shows the film in his or her classroom. The other teacher conducts a make-up work period for students from both classes who have work to complete. Rotate the jobs weekly or monthly between the two teachers. Students who finish their work during the period may **not** see the film; they must stay in the room where the work period is held. Students will be motivated to finish their work during the week in order to see the Friday film.

Progress Reports: Send home daily or weekly progress reports to keep parents posted. Reproducible progress reports are on pages 39 and 40.

QUESTION: *How do you get students to bring notes and papers back to school?*

Award: Give an award to students who bring papers back to school on time. See the list of no-cost rewards on page 61.

Peer Pressure: Use peer pressure techniques! Students can earn points for their team, group or row if everyone brings papers back on time.

Take-to-School Box: Suggest that parents help their children establish a special place at home where they put items that must be brought back to school.

Managing student behavior

QUESTION: *How can you get students to settle down quickly without wasting time?*

The Countdown: Before you begin your first lesson on Monday morning, tell the class that you are giving them 30 minutes of free time which they may claim on Friday afternoon. Write "30 minutes" on the chalkboard. You might want to discuss different options for using the free time and let students take a vote on Friday. Tell the class that when you notice time being wasted unnecessarily, you will say "Countdown." Then you will subtract the number of minutes and seconds that are wasted from 30 minutes. At the end of the week, students decide how to use the remaining time.

Keep a record on the chalkboard.

Monday

The Countdown

minutes	seconds
29	60
—	50
29	10

Gold Medal Group: Divide your class into groups. You can move the desks into clusters or seat students in rows. Give each group a name or number. For example, if you have five groups, assign numbers to each group and write those numbers on the chalkboard. Award points to groups who work quietly, settle down quickly without wasting time after recess or lunch, etc. If three groups come in quietly after recess, give points to all three groups. (If you give points only to the first group that settles down, the activity becomes a race, potentially causing a behavior problem.) Give points to groups when you walk to the library or playground. Just bring along a piece of paper to jot down points. Award points throughout the day. The group that has the most points at the end of the day becomes the "Gold Medal Group" for the next day. This group has privileges such as lining up first, first to get materials, etc. Start with a blank slate each day and begin awarding points again.

Write on chalkboard.

Gold Medal
#1 — 5+1+2
#2 — 6+2
#3 — 5+2
#4 — 1+2
#5 — 5+2

Tips for using the Gold Medal Group idea:

• Never take points away.

• Make sure the groups are balanced. If all the talkative students are together, that group will give up because they won't have a chance to win.

• Experiment to see if this idea works better on a daily or weekly basis in your classroom. A daily, immediate reward tends to be more effective with younger and less mature students.

Rewards your students will love

Rewards for Individual Students

Remember . . .

- Rewards should be earned.
- Rewards are not meaningful if given too liberally.
- The reward is more self-enhancing if selected by the student. Consider making a Reward Chart and posting it on a classroom wall. You can give students choices by asking if they want reward number two or number seven. (See the list of no-cost rewards on page 61.)
- Tell your class exactly what they must do to earn awards so students will work toward a specific goal. For example, give an award to students who have three perfect spelling tests in a row. The award will be more meaningful than if it was given for every perfect test.
- If you have rubber coin stamps, you can give each child a paper wallet. Stamp the wallet with coin stamps. When the coin stamps add up to a certain amount, the child has earned an award. (You can use a construction paper piggy bank instead of a wallet.)

- Hold a swap meet at the end of the school year. Ask students to bring a used toy, book or game to school. Assign a value for each item. Students use the "money" from their piggy banks or wallets to spend at the swap meet.
- Make a coupon book of awards that students can earn. Use the reproducible coupon book on page 60.

My Coupon Book

Name _____

Be first in line.

Ten minutes of free time.

Get a drink of water.

Work at the teacher's desk.

Be a messenger.

Instant help from the teacher.

Sharpen one pencil.

FS-8302 Instant Idea Book

No-cost rewards

- When you want to give your students a "gift," look at your award list for ideas. For example, cut out 30 pink hearts and write "Ten Minutes Free Time" on each one. Give a heart to every student for Valentine's Day. (Tip: Make sure students write their names on award coupons.)

10 minutes FREE time

No-Cost Awards: List and post in your classroom.

AWARDS:

1. Be first in line.
2. Take care of the class pet.
3. Lead an activity.
4. Play with clay.
5. One free homework assignment.
6. Choose a story for the teacher to read.
7. Choose a game for the class to play.
8. Use a timer while you work at your desk.
9. Have your work checked instantly by the teacher.
10. Get instant help from the teacher.
11. Take 10 minutes of free time.
    Set a timer for 10 minutes so you know when time is up.
12. Be a messenger.
13. Have a private talk with the teacher.
14. Keep the class mascot (a stuffed animal) on your desk for one day.
15. Read a story to the kindergarten class.
16. Read a story to the principal.
17. Select an award certificate. (Duplicate assortment of certificates and mount them on wallpaper samples so they are available for student selection.)
18. Help another teacher for 15 minutes.
19. Watch a film in another classroom.
20. Ask your teacher to eliminate one of your grades from the grade book.
21. Help your teacher teach a lesson.
22. Help your teacher correct papers.
23. Work at your teacher's desk.
24. Observe the class pet for 10 minutes.
25. Listen to a record or tape through a headset.
26. Watch a filmstrip.
27. Go to the media center.
28. Write on the teacher's chalkboard.
29. Select an item from the Prize Box (a collection of free goodies that you keep in the closet). Start collecting items such as date books from stationery stores, balloons, pencils, key chains, etc. Look for these items at teacher conventions, new store or bank openings, inside cereal boxes, etc.

FS-8302 Instant Idea Book